101 DRUM TIPS

STUFF ALL THE PROS KNOW AND USE

BY SCOTT SCHROEDL

Recording Credits

The audio CD was recorded, mixed, and mastered at The Dream Factory in Madison, WI.
Drums, Scott Schroedl
Engineer, Jake Johnson
www.scottschroedl.com

ISBN 0-634-05342-6

7777 W. BLUEMOUND RD. P.O. BOX 13819 MILWAUKEE, WI 53213

In Australia Contact:
Hal Leonard Australia Pty. Ltd.
22 Taunton Drive P.O. Box 5130
Cheltenham East, 3192 Victoria, Australia
Email: ausadmin@halleonard.com

Visit Hal Leonard Online at
www.halleonard.com

TABLE OF CONTENTS

① WARMING UP

Whether playing a gig or doing a recording session, always try to warm up first. Think about it: Runners stretch and jog slowly before sprinting their fastest. It makes sense to warm up and stretch the muscles before a hard-hitting gig. (I've heard horror stories of drummers on tour who didn't warm up at all before hitting the stage and playing an intense show. Later, it caught up with them as they experienced all sorts of wrist and arm problems.)

A thorough warm-up is especially advisable under the adverse conditions of "the road"—like loading into a club when the temperature outside is below freezing, or waiting for show time when the air conditioning is cranked, making the muscles stiff. If this is the case, you can expose your hands and forearms under warm to hot water (don't burn yourself!) to increase blood flow and to begin warming up the muscles. This doesn't replace warming up with sticks in your hands, but it does help you get started.

I typically spend anywhere between fifteen minutes to a half an hour warming up before a gig. I'll play through a bunch of different rudiments that really work the fingers and wrists. (I carry a practice pad along to warm up on my own without disturbing anyone.) Some of my favorites are double-stroke and single-stroke rolls, paradiddles, and flam accents. They look like this:

TRACK 1

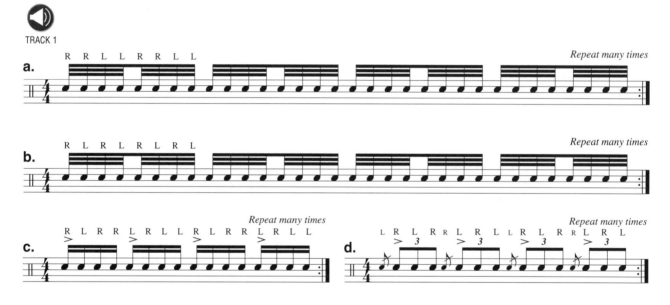

You can also link rudiments together for a great exercise, like this:

TRACK 2

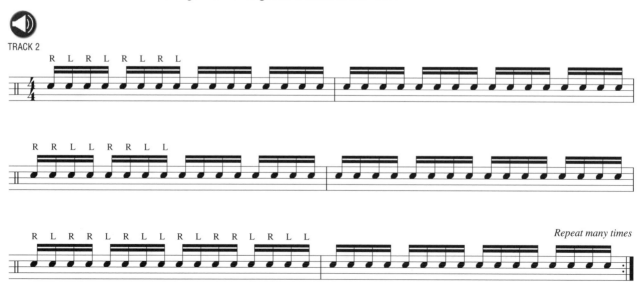

Here are three of my favorite warm-ups:

2 YOUR DRUM CARPET

First of all, it's a good idea to have a carpet on which you can set up your drums to prevent them from sliding away. Ever tried setting up on a wood or tile floor? Chances are that you found your bass drum and hi-hat a foot away from you before you even came to the first chorus of the opening tune. When playing a new place, you never know whether or not the stage will be carpeted, so bring your own.

Since you'll be carrying your own carpet to every gig, why not use it to help you set up faster? I like to mark on my carpet where everything touches it. For instance, I'll use either a permanent marker or small strips of duct tape around the hardware tripod bases, bass drum spurs, the back of the bass drum and hi-hat pedals—even where my stool goes—to set up quicker. I'd suggest setting up on your carpet for a few days when practicing and making adjustments to your kit before permanently marking your carpet. Once everything is where you want it and you've marked it, your kit will set up exactly the same way every gig (providing you also follow Tip #3).

③ MARKING YOUR HARDWARE

It's also important to mark your hardware so that it, too, sets up the same every time. Most stands now come with "memory locks." If some pieces of your stand don't come with these memory locks, you may be able to find them as after-market add-ons. Take your stand along to the drum shop to make sure these memory locks fit.

If you can't find memory locks to fit certain stands, you can also use a permanent marker to mark the tubing for height adjustments, tilter angles, etc. (Some boom stands contain up to four separate pieces. Many times, you need to break each stand down that far in order to get them into a hardware case!) To keep all of the parts organized, try color-coding your stands with colored electrical tape—use the red tape for all the pieces of your ride stand, blue for the crash stand, etc. You can also number your different stands with the numbers electricians use to label wires.

④ MIRROR, MIRROR...

Use a mirror when practicing. Purchase the inexpensive types (around $10) that are made to mount on the back of a door. They're about one foot by four feet. Lean them up against the wall in your practice room. If you can afford it, get two.

The mirrors are to help you realize things such as your posture, technique, sticking heights, etc. Even if you're practicing on a practice pad, set up the mirror directly in front of you. You may notice your shoulders are shrugged due to tension while playing, some of your fingers are coming off of the sticks (not being used), etc.

The main thing I've learned when using mirrors for practice is, they help me to play more relaxed. The first time I set them up while playing to a favorite CD, I watched myself while playing. When it came time to play a difficult fill, I noticed the tension in my face and shoulders. Needless to say, the fill didn't come out smoothly. I backed up the CD and played it again, watching myself now playing more relaxed. Of course, I now played the fill perfectly.

Watch the pros play, and you'll notice that they are always relaxed!

5 GETTING HEARD

If your band is playing larger clubs and festivals where your drums need to be amplified, take your own mics, cables, and mic stands.

If the sound company you are using has better stuff, use theirs. Sometimes, you never know what you're going to have until you get there. It's always better to be prepared than to be sorry you weren't.

I've been in situations, when opening for national bands, where I had to use my own mics in order to be heard properly. Had I not brought my own, I would have had to settle for a crappy kick mic and an over-head to cover quite a large kit—just because the sound guy was too lazy to go through the trouble of switching the mics over.

6 THE BASS DRUM BEATER

Believe it or not, the bass drum beater has a lot to do with the feel and sound of your bass drum. Some beaters feel heavier than others due to more mass on the end of the shaft. You can also add adjustable weights to the shaft to give you even more weight if you so desire.

The material of the beater head also affects the sound. Listen to this demo to hear first a felt beater and then a hard plastic one.

TRACK 4

Years ago, there were mainly only felt beaters. Now there are many more options available, such as plastic, hard felt, soft felt, wood, and hard rubber. Some manufacturers offer beaters with four different options in one; you just twist the beater a quarter turn to get a different sound. Experiment with different beaters to find one (or more) that best fits your style.

Since the bass drum is hit consistently in the same place, you'll want to protect the head from wearing out prematurely. Heads will dent and wear out quickly; friction causes heat build-up, which will ultimately cause failure of the head. There is quite a range of materials used to make protective patches. Some patches do alter the initial attack, but generally they add longevity to a bass drum head. They usually come sized for use with a single pedal, but are also offered in a wider version to accommodate users of double pedals.

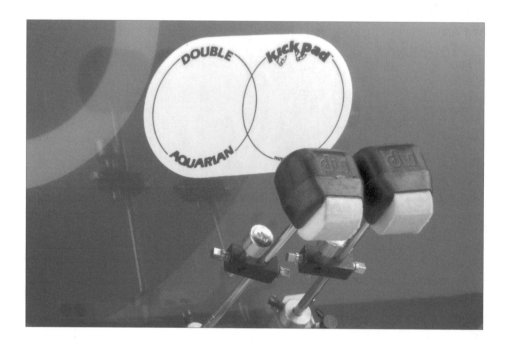

Some patches use a plastic or metal disc to accentuate the attack, or "click," of the hit. The type of patch you use should ultimately be determined by the style of music you play and the sound you're shooting for. I prefer patches that are manufactured specifically for drum heads, but Moleskin Padding by Dr. Scholl's is a readily available, inexpensive alternative that can be purchased at a drugstore.

To install the patches, remove the adhesive backing from the patch and depress the pedal so that the beater almost comes in contact with the head. This is to make sure the beater will hit in the center of the patch, since not all beaters hit exactly in the center of the head. Once it's lined up, stick the patch onto the head, and you're ready to go!

One more tip: don't use duct tape to protect the head from the beater. When the tape begins to wear through, its adhesive will stick to the beater.

8 · THE PACKING LIST

One of the worst things that can happen as a gigging drummer is to forget to pack something important, such as a bass drum pedal or even your sticks. I have a few different set-ups depending on the gig or recording session I'm packing my gear for. To help keep everything straight, I've made a list of things to check off once I've loaded my car for each different scenario. I keep my lists in my Palm Pilot for easy access, but you could just as easily write them out by hand (or print them off your computer, make Xeroxes, etc.).

I typically load my car and then pull out my list to double-check that I have everything. I've listed the items in the order I needed to load them in so I can track myself loading the gear, making sure I have everything. The list also works great at the end of the night when you're loading out after the gig—so you go home with everything you came with.

9 · CARRY YOUR CALENDAR

Carry your calendar with you at all times. If you're a freelance drummer, many times you'll get calls from different players wondering your availability. They'd rather book you on the spot than have to call you back. They might not even call you back if they can get a hold of another, more organized drummer right away.

Sometimes, when you just finish playing to a packed club, the owner will ask to book another show on the spot. You'll be prepared if you've got your calendar with you. It might not be a bad idea to clue your bandmates in on this tip, too.

10 · PRACTICE STICKS

When practicing rudiments or warming up, try using marching sticks to build the strength in the intricate muscles of the hands and arms more quickly. Use these large sticks only on your snare drum or practice pad.

Play a double-stroke roll for five minutes straight, varying the dynamics and speed (see tip #1 for an example of a double-stroke roll). The idea is to increase the strength and dexterity in your fingers. Here is a shortened version of what I'm talking about.

TRACK 5

11 THE SOUND GUY

If you're in a situation where your band uses a large sound system, chances are there will be at least a house engineer and possibly a monitor engineer. These are the people responsible for making you sound good to the audience and to yourself. Be nice to them! It will make your job easier. The more polite you are to the sound guys, the better your monitor mix will likely be!

12 SEEK AND YE SHALL FIND

The next time you're driving your car and there is nothing good on your favorite radio stations, press the seek button. You know the one; it scans until it finds the next strongest signal and plays it for five seconds before moving on. I also like doing this when driving in a city other than where I live. You get to hear many different types of music. When I hear something interesting, I listen longer. It's great for broadening your musical listening, even if it's only for a few seconds at a time.

13 HEARING PROTECTION

You heard it a million times when practicing while you were growing up in your parents' house: "Can't you play any softer?"

If you're going to lay down a killer groove, chances are it's going to be loud enough to damage your hearing in the long run. If you're slamming backbeats on your snare, it's pretty easy to hit 115 decibels from your perspective. According to the OSHA standard, you can only play at that volume for about 5 minutes without risking some kind of hearing loss.

Earplugs come in a few different types and costs. The most basic are the foam type used in industrial situations. They cut down the volume by about 27 decibels. They are cheap and do their job of decreasing volume well, but for many musicians they sound "muddy." You'll notice that your kick and toms sound really cool because of their low frequencies, but you'll overplay your cymbals because the earplugs filter out too many of the high frequencies.

Alternatives to the foam plugs are ones made especially for musicians. They use a special filter that more evenly decreases the volume at all frequencies. One type is a one-size-fits-all, and the other needs custom ear impressions done by an audiologist. They range between 12 and 25 decibels reduction.

It's also a good idea to have your hearing checked once a year. Drummers many times will have more loss in the higher frequencies in their left ear due to playing the hi-hat on that side. When your hearing is gone, it's gone. Take precautionary measures before it's too late.

14 IN-EAR MONITORS

Another great way to protect your hearing and to also hear the band better is to use in-ear monitors. These are little speakers that fit in your ears. They're similar to headphones but much less conspicuous. They come with foam ends for one-size-fits-all or, better yet, custom-molded for a comfortable fit. The custom molds need to be fitted by an audiologist.

Because of the way these monitors fit in your ears, they also reduce the volume around you. You can then hear what you send into the speakers even better. Since you are decreasing the volume around you, there is less of a need to crank the ear monitors up as loud to hear.

In-ear monitors work great for playing live if you have a decent monitoring system. They work equally well in recording situations to keep the click from bleeding into the open microphones. I use mine in both cases, as well as for transcribing music or just listening on a portable CD or mp3 player.

15 THE TWO-DRUM CHALLENGE

If you're like me, at one point in your drumming career you had way too many toms in your set-up—and, of course, you had to fit in as many as you could into every fill. In my case, as I became a more mature player, I used fewer toms, and I realized I could make my fills more interesting by just using better technique and ideas.

Try breaking your kit down to just the basics: kick, snare, one tom, hi-hat, crash, and ride. The idea is to force yourself to play fills using only your snare and one tom. Play a groove, then fill, and keep repeating this.

TRACK 6

Really work on coming up with interesting fills using only these two drums. Think about dynamics, syncopation, and accents. Try using rim shots or any other crazy sounds you can get out of acoustic drums. Later on, you could also incorporate the kick drum into the fills if you wish.

Trust me, your fill ideas will improve. When you get the hang of this, go back to your normal tom setup, but not back to your old ways.

16 BRANCHING OUT

If you're just a drumset player, also learn to play other percussion instruments. The more you can play, the more you're worth to other musicians. For instance, if you get called to play drumset on a recording, mention that you could also spice up the track with percussion if they'd like. Many songs use tambourine, shakers, congas, bongos, etc. All of these, as easy as they may look, require practice on your part to play authentically and smoothly. Put together a bag full of common percussion instruments to take with you to recording sessions.

17 THE BASS DRUM SPURS

When setting up your bass drum, take some time to get the spurs set up correctly. Clamp your pedal on the bass drum hoop. Adjust the spurs on the bass drum so the front hoop is raised off the floor. Raise the drum just enough to slide your fingers under the front hoop, and tighten the spurs, making sure they are even so the drum sits straight.

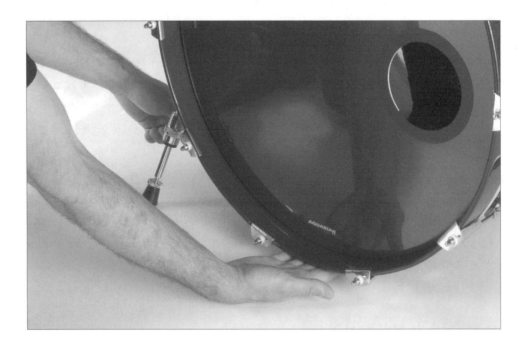

To help prevent the bass drum from sliding forward when playing, most spurs have retractable spikes for use on carpet. Raising the front hoop off the ground affects the feel of the bass drum; the higher you raise the hoop, the shorter the distance between the batter head and the pedal beater.

18 THE HI-HAT TILTER

When setting up your hi-hats, turn the tilter mechanism (it's what the bottom cymbal sits on) towards you; in other words, the screw should be facing the side where you strike the cymbals with your sticks.

Set the angle of the bottom cymbal so that you don't create an air pocket between the cymbals when you step on the pedal. Now that you have the adjustment screw facing where you strike with the stick, the cymbals will hit together sooner when you play an open hi-hat, creating the "sizzle" sound.

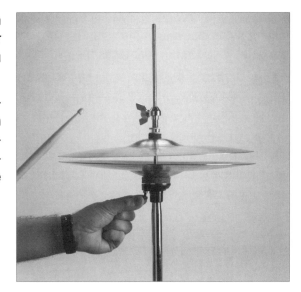

19 ADJUSTING THE BEATER

Adjust the beater height so that it hits close to the middle of the bass drum. This may be impossible on larger (e.g., 24") drums. On smaller 18" bass drums, you may want to purchase a bass drum "lifter" to raise the drum off the ground so the beater can hit closer to the center.

Different types of beaters (felt, plastic, wood) have a different weight to them. The height of the beater also greatly affects the feel of the pedal. If the beater is extended out as far as it will go, but you feel that the throw of the beater still needs more weight, you can purchase small weights that attach to the beater's shaft.

20 HOMEMADE DAMPENERS

Dampening rings are made by a few different manufacturers, and come in different widths and sizes to fit your toms and snare. You can also make some yourself using old single-ply drumheads.

Take an old head that matches the size of the drum you want to muffle. You'll want to carefully cut out the head, right where it flattens out past the collar, and discard the metal ring part of the drumhead. Depending on how much muffling you'd like, measure inwards about three inches from the edge, and cut out the center. You will now have a dampening ring. Place it on your snare (or tom) to test it. If you'd prefer to muffle less, cut more off from the inside of the ring. You could make a bunch to have a selection of different widths (3/4", 1", 1 1/2", 2", etc.).

21 PROTECTING YOUR CYMBALS

I can't tell you how many times I've seen drummers playing pro-quality cymbals but not using cymbal felts or nylon sleeves on their stands. They spend a small fortune on the cymbal itself but don't protect the hole, which in turn damages the cymbal. Over time, the hole will elongate and ruin the cymbal.

Check all of your cymbal stands' felts and nylon sleeves frequently to make sure they're not worn through. Determine if you have all of the proper pieces. Placed first on the tilter should be the cupped metal washer, followed by a thick felt. If the felt is too thin, the metal washer will scrape on the underside of the cymbal when it swings. Next, you should have the nylon sleeve that slips over the threaded metal tilter post. This prevents metal-to-metal contact at the hole of the cymbal, which in turn saves your cymbal investment. Lastly, place another felt on top of the cymbal and tighten down the wing nut to hold everything on.

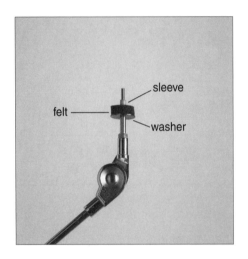
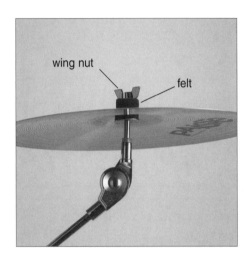

Don't crank the screw down too tightly. Crash and splash cymbals need to be able to swing very freely, not only to ring out but to absorb the shock of the stick striking the cymbal.

22 LIFTING GEAR

Band gear can get quite heavy and cumbersome. Be sure to keep your back straight and lift from your legs. Ask a band mate for assistance on the really big stuff; it's not worth throwing your back out. Purchase a weightlifting belt if you're really serious. The cost of the belt could save you hundreds at the chiropractor. Get a wheeled cart to help move your stuff. You can usually put more on a cart than you can carry, saving trips to your car.

It's also a good idea to load in and out wearing gloves. They will save your precious hands from slivers, cuts, and pinches.

23 DRUM TECH TIPS

If it's your job to set up a drumset for someone else, it will help to take photos of their set-up. Include close-up shots of critical things. If you carry a laptop with you, have the digital photos in there along with any other reminder notes.

This is also a good idea for someone just beginning to gig themselves. Maybe your stuff has been set up at your rehearsal place for so long that it takes you forever to get set up at the gig. If you have a small car and a lot of gear like me, take sequential photos of the packing of your gear into the car.

24 TAKE LESSONS

You are never too old or too good to take lessons. It's true that you may have to find just the right teacher, but in the long run you'll be glad you did.

The purpose of taking lessons is not to show what you know; rather it's to expose what you don't know. The teacher should find your weaknesses and help you develop them into more confident playing.

You may even know exactly what you want to learn from a teacher, like learning to play Latin grooves. Maybe you only need a few lessons to get you on the right track.

25 MUSCLE MEMORY

When learning to play difficult passages, practice them extremely slowly. I've had many students who try to learn something new by playing it way too fast. Needless to say, they never really get it down until they slow down.

Give your limbs a chance to do what your brain is telling them to do. When playing slow, you begin to get the motions into muscle memory. Play the passage slowly a bunch of times, and gradually begin to speed it up until you can play it at the desired tempo. The understanding that you gain by learning something slowly will allow you to play it at unbelievable speeds in the long run.

26 TOOL KIT LIST

- Duct tape—for muffling drums, taping down cords, etc.
- Electrical tape—always handy
- Mag-lite—for dark stages when you lose something
- Screwdrivers—Phillips and flathead, large and small
- Allen wrenches—for adjusting bass drum pedals and to tighten some lugs to the drum shell
- Soldering iron & solder—to fix bad microphone, speaker, and electronic drum cords
- Wire cutters and strippers—you know, to cut and strip wires!
- Zip-ties—many uses
- Band-Aids—you never know
- AA batteries—for some condenser microphones
- Spare cymbal felts, nylon cymbal sleeves, and wing nuts—I always seem to lose them on the dark stage
- WD-40—to lube that squeaky pedal
- Microphone clips—they can break pretty easily on the road
- Battery tester—check to get every last bit of power from your batteries (hey, musicians are cheap!)
- Drum keys—you can never have enough of them around
- Jewelers' screwdrivers—for removing microphone plugs and banana speaker plugs
- Ground lift plugs—if you're using any electronics, you never know when you'll need them to get rid of the hum
- Bass drum beater impact patch—they cut down on wear and tear on the head
- Tension rods with washers—just for spares (check the length needed for the tension rods of your different drums)
- Snare cord or straps—occasionally they break
- Sharpie, pen, and pencil—for making notes on the set list or signing autographs!
- Spare lugs—not very likely you'll need them, but just in case
- Earplugs—for those aggressively amplified gigs
- Superglue—tons of uses
- Swiss army type knife—always handy
- Pliers and adjustable wrench—for loosening tight hardware, etc.
- Microphone ends and 1/4" plugs—spares for microphone and electronic drum cords
- Hi-hat clutch—sometimes they strip out
- Moongel or dampening rings—to get rid of unwanted ring of your drums in the PA
- Razor blade cutters—always handy
- Spare bass drum beater—you never know when the shaft might break
- Lug locks—to keep your tension rods from backing out
- Imodium—the show must go on!
- Throat lozenges—to sooth your throat when singing with a cold
- Pain reliever

See photo on next page.

27 ...AND CARRY A BIG STICK

If you're a rock drummer playing larger-sized toms tuned low, a larger diameter drumstick will produce a deeper, fuller tone than a light stick.

If you tire easily trying to keep up, volume-wise, with the guitarist whose amp is on eleven, larger sticks will also help you to compete.

28 A LITTLE AT A TIME

When it comes time to change drumheads, it's best to loosen each tension rod a little at a time until the rods are completely loose. This keeps the hoop from "giving" too much in one certain area (making it no longer true), and is easier on the drum shell itself. This is especially important on snare drums, where high tension is common.

Snare drums typically use the same lug for the top and bottom head, so if you need to remove the batter, for instance, loosen the tension rods for the snare side a little, too (don't forget to tension them back up after installing the new batter head). This way, you are not pulling the lug (on the shell) one way as hard.

29 THE DANGLING TENSION RODS

When changing drumheads, you don't need to remove the tension rods from the hoop; just let them dangle as you pull the head and hoop off of the drum shell. It's handy to have your drum stool nearby on which to set the old head and hoop; the tension rods can just hang over the stool.

30 GOT A HOLE IN YOUR HEAD?

A hole cut into the resonant head usually has two purposes. The first is to allow for a microphone to be placed inside the drum—either for recording, or for amplification through a live performance sound system. In live performance, when using a microphone on a stand in front of your bass drum, be careful to place it so that your guitarist or singer doesn't accidentally kick it and tear the head (which they're notorious for doing).

The second purpose of the hole is to let the air escape from inside the drum. When you use a full front head, the air can't escape, except through the small air vent in the shell. When playing with a full front head, you may experience the pedal beater bouncing back off of the batter head. If your technique is to "bury the beater," you might find this set-up frustrating. You could try loosening the batter head until it almost wrinkles, or you could cut a small hole in the resonant head to allow the air to escape. To still get a sound similar to that of a full front head, cut a five-inch hole, off-center, about two and one-half inches from the edge.

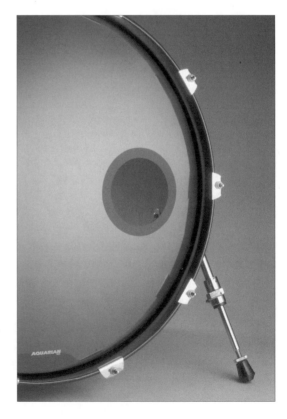

Many drumhead manufacturers offer resonant heads with pre-cut holes as part of their product line. If you'd prefer not to spend the extra money, and cut the full head you've got, here are a few tips. Find something with which to trace the hole on the head—a small splash cymbal, coffee can, CD, or anything else that is round and the appropriate size. Some manufacturers have pre-made templates for this, too. After determining where on the head you'd like the hole, use a felt-tip pen to trace the object on the inside of the head. Place the head on cardboard, or something else you can cut into (when the razor blade goes through the head, you don't want to cut your carpet or Mom's new linoleum). With the razor blade, begin cutting out the hole. Take your time, and be very careful not to cut outside the line. If anything, cut in toward the center. If you slip and cut outward, the head may tear easily once you begin playing.

There is another trick for making a hole—one that definitely requires adult supervision, and I claim no responsibility for misuse. Find a coffee or some other type of can to match the size of the hole you'd like. Heat your stove burner on high, and place the empty can on the burner to heat it up. The bass drum head should be off of the drum and placed on concrete—such as a garage floor or sidewalk—with the outside of the head facing up. Remove the heated can from the burner with pliers, and carefully lower it onto the head at the desired place. If the can is hot enough, it should melt a perfect hole through the head. Let the head cool for a few minutes before putting it on your bass drum.

31 PACKING SPRING LUGS

Many of the older or more inexpensive drums of today are likely to get a rattling sound from spring-loaded lugs.

This problem is most discouraging when in a recording session, since most drum recordings of today involve close miking. You may want to remove the cymbals from your drum set in order to more clearly hear your drums and listen for lug rattle. Sometimes, you may be fooled by rattles that are not due to lugs—such as the sound of a washer on a loose tension rod, or the spiked end of bass drum spurs with retractable rubber feet. If you are using the spiked end, make sure to thread the rubber end all the way back, so that it's tight and won't rattle.

If you do detect a rattle coming from a lug, you can quiet the noise by packing it. The best way to do this is to wrap the spring with either felt or cotton cloth. First, remove the heads and all of the lugs. Carefully remove the spring (it's under tension, and might shoot out) from the lug. Cut felt or cotton cloth so that it wraps around the spring, covering the width of the space within the lug where the spring sits—keeping in mind that when the spring is not compressed inside the lug, it's longer.

Replace the lug on the drum and tighten it back on. Be sure not to over-tighten, as that could break the lug.

Just in case, you may as well pack all of your drums' lugs to avoid future problems. Nothing is more disheartening in a recording session than when you think all of your drums are tuned and you're ready to go, and then the engineer hears a rattle from your drums—and you spend an hour trying to find it.

32 STAYING IN TUNE

Drumheads stretch, although they do so mostly within the first few hours of playing (then they begin to wear out where hit). Often, it is easy to mistake the head stretching for the detuning effect. But in reality, the tension rods loosen up from vibrations when the drum is played, which is a common cause of your drum going out of tune. There have been several products designed to help prevent this problem:

- One of these is a nut that threads on the tension rod before you thread it into the lug. Once the drum is tuned, you would spin this nut down onto the lug, which helps to hold it in place.

- Index Tension Tuners are replacement tension rods that use miniature ball bearings to create clicks as you turn them, which help to keep the rods from backing out.

- Lug Locks are my favorite; they consist of a piece of plastic with a hole, which you press down over the head of the tension rod. The hole forms to the shape of the tension rod head. If the rod begins to back out, the Lug Lock hits the hoop of the drum to stop it.

You can use any of these different products on your toms and snares. Typically, the snare drum will need it the most. I install Lug Locks on my snare drum batter side, on the four lugs closest to me (in other words, where the sticks come in contact with the hoop during rim shots).

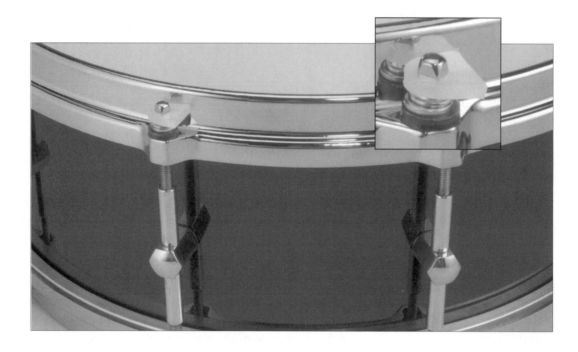

Sometimes during hard playing, the snare-side (bottom) tension rod closest to where I play rim shots loosens up and falls out of the hoop—if I haven't also put a Lug Lock there.

33 SUSPENSION MOUNTS

Prior to the '80s, tom mount brackets were always attached directly to the shell. Some even had the tom arms protruding through the shell. You may already know that the more mass attached to the shell, the less freely it will vibrate. And certainly, a hole in the shell can't be good for sustain, either. So, to bring out the drums' natural sustain, Gary Gauger invented a suspension system called Resonance Isolation Mounting System, or RIMS for short. This component allowed the tom mount bracket to be removed from the shell altogether, and attach instead to the RIMS unit, which suspended the drum through the tension rods—allowing the shell to resonate freely.

Many drum manufacturers now include their own versions of RIMS, mostly on their high-end drums; but retrofit mounts are available for use on any brand and quality of drums today. So, to get the most open sustain out of your toms, add suspension mounts to them.

34 TIMING IS EVERYTHING

Your role as a drummer is first and foremost to keep good time. Your flashy fills may impress some people, but to get (and keep) a good gig, you'll need to have good time.

Buy a metronome and practice with it. It is always a struggle at first (and a real eye-opener) when you realize your grooves or fills speed up throughout the course of a song.

For drummers, I recommend a metronome that has an earphone jack built in—so that you'll be able to hear the click over the sound of your drums.

If your band is preparing to go into a recording studio for the first time, it's a good idea to rehearse with a metronome. This early preparation for the studio will save a lot of frustration, time, and money in the long run. Keep in mind, as the drummer, you may be the only one to hear the click—so if the rest of the band is rushing the tempo, you'll need to hold them back.

35 COUNT OUT LOUD

When practicing something new or unusual, count out loud to better understand tricky rhythms. The more senses you use, the better you comprehend and the quicker you learn new rhythms. This is also helpful when transcribing difficult music (especially in odd time signatures).

36 THE EXTERNAL CLOCK

To help with my internal time, I also like to keep time with my left heel (hi-hat foot). This involves silently tapping my heel on the hi-hat pedal with the cymbals closed. The object is not to make a sound, but rather to have an external limb keeping time. Of course, you could also keep time using the hi-hat where it could sound effective with the music.

37 BALANCE

As a drummer, you might think your instrument is the drumset. In fact, you're really playing a variety of separate instruments. Each requires a different touch or feel. Metal instruments such as cymbals and cowbells have virtually no "give" compared to a loosely tuned snare, bass drum, or tom.

So when playing your drumset, make sure you have a good balance volume-wise between all of your limbs and the instruments they play. The object is to make the collection of separate instruments making up your drumset to sound as one complete unit without something sticking out like a sore thumb.

38 RELAX!

When I began playing gigs in front of people in a band situation, the tendency more often than not was to feel nervous. To help calm my nerves, I wrote "Relax" on a small piece of paper and taped it to one of my tom rims just over the snare drum. It became a constant reminder to stay focused and to relax my body. I also found it helpful to take deep calming breaths to ease tension.

When you play more relaxed, everything tends to sound more fluid and controlled. Being well prepared for the gig will help for starters, but try my little note trick, or think of your own.

39 RECORD YOUR PRACTICING

Recording your practice session is a great way to hear your weaknesses and track your progress when learning something new. Even a simple tape recorder will work. Review the tape to listen constructively for the consistencies (or inconsistencies) in your playing. It's easier to critique yourself when listening back with an open mind than when things are happening on the spot. Sometimes, what you thought was the coolest fill when you played it may not sound so cool upon second listen. Conversely, you may have played something interesting by accident, and you'll have it on tape to review and build on.

You can always take this recording idea to the next level and record or videotape your band rehearsing or playing live. I know that I've personally gained so much valuable insight into my own playing with this simple technique.

40 EYE CONTACT

When playing in a live situation, make sure you set up so that you can see all of the other band members easily. As the drummer, you unfortunately can't move much when seated at your drums, so making eye contact easily is very important.

Decide on who will be in charge of cueing the changes, and be watching for them attentively. If you are the one cueing, do it consistently the same way every time (one or two bars before the change). Use bigger arm motions (to cue a ritard ending, for instance) or even that certain look to help everyone change at the correct time.

41 POSTURE

When playing drumset, be sure to sit up straight on the stool. Drummers are notorious for having bad backs (partly due to lugging around heavy gear). Drumming is quite demanding on your spine since your arms are constantly reaching out and your feet are dancing on the pedals, making it difficult to get constant support on the stool. You might want to try a drum stool that has a backrest attached to it. I began using one about ten years ago, and I love it. It gives me great lower- and mid-back support. Even if you don't want to lean back constantly while playing, you could still use it to give your back a short break between songs.

42 YOUR PRACTICE SPACE

This is a room in which you'll be spending a lot of time, and you should set it up to make it not only comfortable but functional. Select a room that will aid in keeping the volume down for your neighbors and family. A basement is a good choice because it's typically underground and has few, if any, windows. If you're gigging and have to move your drums in and out frequently, also consider accessibility for convenient loading.

Set up your space so that you have easy access to the things you'll need for effective practicing: CD player, CDs, cassette player, closed-ear headphones, sturdy music stand, drum lesson books, metronome, earplugs, inexpensive recording device, etc. If you have a computer, you may want to use it to play to MP3s or programmed loops.

The room itself should have good lighting. Set up your drums on a large piece of carpet to keep them from sliding around (this helps make the room less ambient, too). A large mirror comes in handy to watch your movements while playing. Hang inspirational pictures or posters on the walls for the finishing touches.

43 DYNAMICS

If you don't play at different dynamic levels, your drumming could be compared to someone speaking in a monotone—not much fun to listen to, is it?

As a drummer, you're able to produce a wide dynamic range, from a whisper to a roar. A great song should take you through peaks and valleys. Even when playing a fill, the interjection of accented notes helps to make the fill sound more interesting—as well as the song as a whole.

44 TEXTURES

Over the years, there have been a lot of new types of sticks, brushes, and mallets created by various companies. These new (and old) drumming tools can be used to create quite a vast array of different sounding textures on the same old drums and cymbals. Next time you're trying to find just the right groove for your latest song, reach down deep into your bag for something other than sticks.

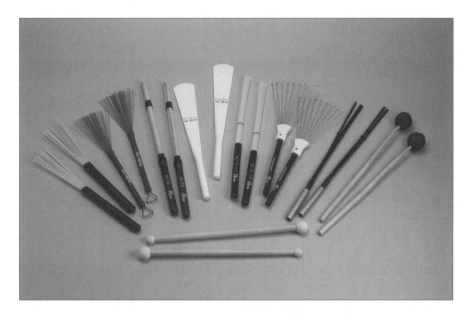

We all know how wire brushes sound, but how about the newer plastic-bristle type? There are quite a few different varieties of multi-rod (thin wood dowels wrapped together) to choose from, too. Some of the more obscures models include bamboo, plastic tubes, or even built-in rattlers. Give them a try; they might be just what you were looking for to create a new sound for yourself. You could even try something different in each hand.

45 ELECTRONIC DRUMS

OK, the purists out there will say "no way," but the reality is that if you have no knowledge of electronic drums in this day and age, you'll be missing out on opportunities. So much modern music uses loops, samples, and sound effects that it's hard to get by without getting into electronic drums to some degree or another. It's common to see a full acoustic drumset with electronic pads intertwined so the drummer can cover the new, more eccentric drum parts. Electronic drums also make a great practice set at home (to keep the volume down for family and neighbors).

SET PLAYING GOALS

If you don't know where you're going, how do you expect to get there? Goal setting is a way to organize your thoughts and actions in order to reap a reward. Start by thinking of your long-range goals, like playing Madison Square Garden, for instance. If you've just begun playing, that's quite a long way off. You need to break things down into short-range goals. Think of it as steps. Your long-range goal is the top of the stairs, short-range goals are quite a few steps in between, and immediate goals are where you get started. An immediate goal might be to set up a regular productive practice schedule. A short-range goal could be to start playing with a band on a smaller club circuit. Everyone's goals are different. Decide on your plan, and follow it to the top!

47 SNARE TENSION ADJUSTMENT

Adjusting the snare tension is a tuning practice often overlooked by inexperienced drummers. Some drummers believe it's either on or off, but the sweetest part of tuning a snare drum is getting the snare tension to work with the tension of the bottom (snare side) head.

Adjust the snare tension using the knob on the strainer. Always adjust this with the throw-off in the off position; then turn it on again, and test the drum by hitting the batter head. As you begin to tighten the bottom head, the snares will loosen, and you'll need to adjust them accordingly. Tensioning the snares is also a personal thing. To test the snare sensitivity, have the snares on, play very softly in the center of the batter head, and listen.

If they tend to rattle too much, you'll need to tighten them up. Track 7 demonstrates the sound of snares that are too loose.

TRACK 7

If your snare drum sounds too tom-like or choked, the snares may be too tight. For a choked snare example, listen to Track 8.

TRACK 8

The snares should sound good when hit very softly or very hard, as demonstrated on Track 9.

TRACK 9

Some drummers adjust their drum's snare tension to fit the style of music they're playing. As an example, blues drummers might want the snares a little looser to sound "fatter," while a pop drummer might want them tighter and more articulate. Just use your best judgment, and don't tighten or loosen the snares to the extremes.

If you are a light hitter, you can have a fairly medium tension on the snare-side head. The harder you play, the tighter you'll need to make the snare-side head. When you hit the snare drum batter head, it forces a column of air down towards the snare-side head. If the snare-side head is loose, and you hit the batter head hard, the snare-side head moves a greater distance than it would when tighter. Keep in mind that the snares will also be forced to stretch along with the head. If they do, the drum will then sound less articulate and sloppier.

48 SNARE DRUM SELECTION

You can't achieve every possible sound using just a single snare drum—even with different tunings and head combinations. In other words, if you have a 6$\frac{1}{2}$" deep, wood-shell snare drum, you won't get it to sound very close to a 3$\frac{1}{2}$" deep, brass-shell snare.

If you play in a band that specializes in one genre of music, this might not be an issue for you; you may be able to get by with one snare drum that fits that style. However, if you're a studio drummer who's called upon to play most anything, you'll need a selection of snares. Studio drummers may take as few as three snares or as many as twenty to a session just to have a choice to find the sound best suited for the song.

49 PLAYING FOR THE SONG

OK, so you've been locked away in your practice space for months working on your four-way independence and Neil Peart fills in order to better yourself as a player. There's nothing wrong with that. Everyone needs to grow. But knowing when to use your new chops is the trick. If you are playing in a Top-40 band, you probably won't need to access your new knowledge of playing in 11/16 time. In other words, play what's required to make the song groove and feel good.

You'd be surprised by the monster chops that some drummers actually have in reserve—because they deceivingly play just what's needed for the song. The key idea is to be over-prepared for anything you intend to play, but use only what's necessary to make the song sound great.

50 FINDING THE RIGHT CYMBAL

Selecting cymbals is a very personal thing. Everyone has different tastes in sounds. If you're playing different styles of music, you may also need different cymbal setups. It's always difficult to walk into a store and find just the sound you're looking for. The environment is different, and you have no real reference to your other cymbal sounds, except what you remember.

When I worked in a music store, I would always encourage drummers to bring their whole cymbal setup along with them when trying to find another sound to complement their existing cymbals. Sometimes, you can set up your current cymbals on a drumset at the store along with the new ones you're auditioning to see how they "fit" in. Put the new cymbal where you intend to have it on your kit; you hear cymbals differently at different heights and placements. Really listen to determine if the new cymbal complements your other cymbals.

If you are trying out ride cymbals, bring your own sticks, too. The tip and size of the drumstick really affect the sound when playing on the ride, so bring what you're used to playing with.

51 DRUMMER HEADPHONES

When practicing along with CDs or a metronome, it's best to use closed-back headphones. Drums are naturally a loud instrument; the closed-back headphones allow you to hear the sounds in the phones rather than so much of the drums around you.

Vic Firth (the drumstick manufacturer) makes drummer's stereo isolation headphones. These are a version of closed-back headphones, but hold tighter to the wearer's head, giving 24 decibels of isolation. Use them to hear the music better, or just to help save your hearing.

52 WATCH AND LISTEN

Today, there are so many opportunities to learn new drumming skills. New videos and DVDs are being released regularly in the music instructional field—a boon to "visual" learners. It's like having a private lesson with a drumming great, and you can review it as many times as you wish!

If you can read music, there are drum books available on just about every facet imaginable. For the cost of one private lesson, you could buy four new books that will keep you busy "woodshedding" your craft for months.

If your local music store sponsors drum clinics, go to them! It's a great way to see the pros up close and be able to ask them questions.

53 CHART READING

When playing for recording sessions, theater work, and some pick-up gigs, you may find yourself having to read a chart. A chart is a musical road map for a song. Most often, very little is written out for drums. Rather, it's mostly guidelines left up to your own interpretation. The things that are usually revealed will be tempo markings, musical style (rock 'n' roll, medium swing, rhumba, etc), song sections, beginning (pick-up notes), ending, musical kicks, and specific full-band rhythms or breaks. Playing a song from a chart requires a previous working knowledge of the general style and its characteristics.

When viewing a chart for the first time, scan it over quickly to take in the general form. If you're playing this on a gig, you'll only have one shot to get it right. If you're in a recording session and can take more than one pass, jot down some quick notes on the chart, after the first run-through, of things you may have learned.

Drummers who've learned to play primarily from written music (orchestral, rudimental, or drumset) can be bewildered when faced with playing from a chart for the first time; it's a new challenge and in some way requires a different set of musical skills. The best preparation is to listen to and learn the general characteristics of as many styles as you can.

54 GROOVING WITH THE CLICK

The click track is basically another term for a metronome when used in a recording situation. Many drummers first encounter a click track when entering a studio for the first time. This can be a horrifying situation unless you've spent time practicing with one.

As you may know, a click track plays "clicks" evenly spaced at a desired tempo. It's one thing to play right on the click, but as you become more comfortable, you can play *around* the click as well. For a laid-back feel, you would play behind each click slightly. For a pushing feel, you would play slightly ahead of the beat. I'm not talking about rushing the tempo three beats per minute, but rather dragging or anticipating each click slightly. The tempo really stays the same, but the feeling is laid back or pushing.

TRACK 10

Listen to this demo to hear the groove first behind the beat, then on the beat, and then ahead of the beat (for four measures each). A cymbal crash sparates each feel. The sequence then repeats, so listen closely to the drastic difference in playing ahead of the beat to playing behind the beat on the repeat.

All of these "feels" could happen in the same song. The verse could be laid back, the bridge right on the beat, and the chorus pushing to add excitement. Then when you come back to the laid-back verse, it feels more relaxed again.

Spend some quality time with your metronome, and explain it to your band mates, too, so they can get into the groove as well.

55 LEARN THE RUDIMENTS

Rudiments to drums are like scales on the piano. If you know them well, you gain much more control and have more "ideas" to draw from.

There are 26 standard American rudiments, but in 1988 the Percussive Arts Society formulated 40 international rudiments. These rudiments were originally written for the snare drum, but can be adapted to drumset playing.

It is always important to master the basics. This is where it all begins. It might be wise to find a qualified teacher to help you learn the rudiments correctly. The object is to play them as cleanly as possible at any tempo.

56 MENTAL PRACTICING

When you just can't sit down at your drumset to practice, try mental practicing. You can "air drum," or just imagine yourself going through the motions. "Hear" the drums and cymbals even though you're really not playing. Think in detail every motion it takes to play a particular beat or song. This kind of practicing helps you really focus on every aspect of your playing. You can even do it while listening to the radio in your car.

I've had a couple of leg surgeries and had to take some time off from practicing on my drumset. Mental practicing helped me keep my mind sharp. Once I had use of my leg again, I really only needed to get the strength and technique back.

I truly believe that if you can clearly "hear" something in your mind, you'll be able to play it. This goes for speed also. The physical technique may be slightly limiting at first, but you'll be on your way much faster.

57 LOST DRUM KEY?

If you're like most drummers, you have a tendency to lose your drum key from time to time. It usually happens when the lights are out on stage and you happen to drop it when you really need it.

I bought this spiraled key chain thing. I attach the drum key on one end, and the other end clips to the floor tom tension rod. When I need to tune, it stretches to reach the snare and all of the toms without ever unhooking it from the floor tom.

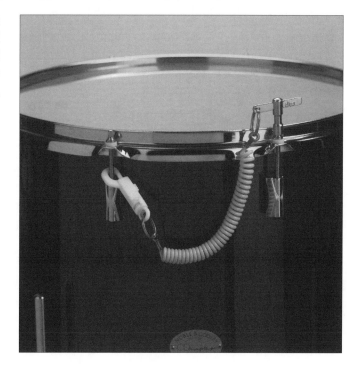

58 BETTER POSITIONING

When setting up your drums, try to position everything within easy reach. Keep the components of your kit as close together as possible. Do you really need your cymbals way up in the air, or the rack toms mounted totally flat? It may look cool, but it will slow you down on those fast fills. The idea is to keep everything close together, so you can get around the drums and cymbals faster, with less effort or wasted motion.

59 THE FULL-TIME MUSICIAN

Just about every young drummer, at one time or another, has dreamed of making it big as a well-known superstar—recording hit albums, touring the world, having your very own drum tech… It could happen, but you can still make a good living doing what you love without being a superstar.

Being a full-time musician just means that everything you do is related to music. Of course, you can still play in your band at night or on the weekends, but what about the rest of the day (or your nights off)? The following list should give you some good ideas on where to start.

- Be the booking agent for your band or others.
- Know something about sound systems? Try mixing for other bands.
- Teach private lessons to up-and-comers.
- Got some recording experience? Try breaking into the jingle business.
- Play on local songwriters' albums.
- Know how to read and write music? Try freelancing as a transcriber for different music publishing companies.
- How about writing drum-related articles for drum magazines? Or writing instructional books? (You could either self-publish them or pitch them to a larger publisher.)

You see that there are quite a few of opportunities out there if you just put your mind to it. Working as a full-time musician can be very rewarding even if you aren't a household name.

60 GET A GRIP!

There are two basic ways to hold your sticks: matched grip and traditional grip.

matched   traditional

Both grips can be used to play any style of music. It basically comes down to your own preference. Many jazz purists will strictly play traditional, and many rockers will play matched, but there really are no rules.

Matched grip is easier to learn since the technique for both hands is the same. For matched grip, the stick will pivot between your thumb and the first joint of your index finger. Grip it about 1/3 from the butt end. The other fingers then wrap loosely around the stick for control.

When playing traditional grip, the right hand grip is exactly like the matched grip. The left hand is a little more difficult. Begin by placing the stick in the "V" between your thumb and index finger about 1/3 from the butt end of the stick, and squeeze together. This is the fulcrum or pivot point for the left hand. The stick will then rest on the ring finger with the pinky underneath for support. Wrap your index finger over the stick and close the circle around the stick by placing the thumb on the index finger. The middle finger more or less acts as a guide for the stick.

If you decide to play with this grip, you may want to reposition your snare drum at an angle to accommodate this different striking angle of the left stick.

When playing the snare drum in front of you, your sticks should form a 90° angle, or slightly less. Just don't bring your hands in too close together, or the range of motion in your wrists will decrease. This will result in less power and speed in the long run. Try both of these grips, and decide which works better for you.

61 BASS DRUM FOOT TECHNIQUE

There are two fundamental ways of playing the bass drum. One is with your foot flat on the pedal; the other is with your heel up.

foot flat

heel up

When playing with your foot flat, you're using just your ankle to propel the beater into the head. When playing with your heel up, you'll use your whole leg, pivoting from the hip. Many rock drummers prefer the "heel up" approach to get more volume out of the drum, but if you're looking for more finesse, try the other way. Some drummers use both techniques depending on the style of music or dynamic level they're playing.

62 OPEN/CLOSED BASS DRUM TONE

The bass drum sounds different depending on the technique you use when striking the head.

For a solid "thump" or closed sound, try holding the beater into the head until right before playing the next note. This technique works best when playing with your heel up. Be careful that you don't let the beater "chatter" against the head. To avoid this, you'll have to hold the pedal down hard. It may also help if you have at least a small hole cut in the front head to allow the air to escape from the drum.

TRACK 11

For a more open sound, let the bass drum beater bounce back immediately after contacting the head. This allows the drumhead to sustain naturally. This is easier to control using the heel down approach. This technique is very popular with jazz drummers who play a smaller bass drum and use it more for "kicks" than to groove.

TRACK 12

Try both ways to explore the uses for playing different styles.

63 CHECKING THE BEARING EDGES

The bearing edge is a very important factor in drum sound and tuning. The bearing edge is either end of the cylindrical drum shell—the only point at which the drumhead touches the shell.

The bearing edge must be perfectly true in order for the head to seat properly, and for the drum to be tuned to its full potential. Every time you change heads, check the condition of the bearing edge for nicks, divots, or rough spots. If you want to check to see that they are totally flat, remove the heads from the drum. Place the shell on a flat surface (we're talking a slab of granite here) and shine a light down into the drum. If the edge is uneven, you will see the light shining from under the shell. If you notice any irregularities, you can have these edges re-cut by a professional. There are two bearing edge cuts. The first, in modern drums, is typically a 45° chamfer cut on the inside bearing edge, which ensures the best trade-off between attack and overall tone. The second cut is a round-over cut, which is the outside cut of the bearing edge, located where the collar of the drumhead contacts the shell. Sometimes this outside cut is also 45°, which increases sustain, as the sharper edge leaves less contact area with the head.

chamfer cut

round-over cut

Many vintage drum shells have nothing more than a wide, round-over cut, which produces less attack and sustain, and gives the impression of more overall warmth, because more area is touching the head.

64 PLAY FROM INSIDE

It's great to practice all kinds of technical things out of books, but what it really comes down to when making music with others is to play with emotion from inside youself. Reading music can often sound mechanical; sometimes, it's great to just play anything you feel. This can be a great release (emotionally) for you.

All difference types of feelings can be relayed through music. For example, you could play aggressively, uncertain, lazy, excited, happy, angry, etc. Really play what the song is about and notice how your playing can affect the other musicians and the song as a whole.

65 STICKING PRINCIPLES

Good sticking is designed to help you play cleanly and easily—and to get you moving around the drums more quickly.

First, imagine you're playing alternating sixteenth notes beginning with your right stick:

Now, for these next fills, keep that same sticking pattern (RLRL); however, if a note is skipped, so is its corresponding hand. You can try "air drumming" these hands if you like (play in the air, but don't hit anything) to keep the alternating sixteenths flowing, or not. This may seem awkward at first, but if you understand the principle, your drumming will be greatly enhanced.

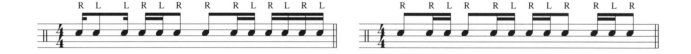

The exception to the above "alternating sixteenths" rule is when playing consecutive eighth notes in a fill. Just alternate hands for the eighths, and then go back to alternating sixteenths:

Are you wondering why all of these fills lead with the right hand? Most fills are played around the toms from left to right (for a right-handed player), and leading with the right hand helps eliminate your sticks from crossing over. Try applying these patterns to snare and toms, and see what happens. Don't be afraid to experiment; practice leading fills with your left hand, too. Remember: when mixing up snare and toms, you may need to try different stickings to make the fill work. Practice until you find the most logical order.

66 THE RIDE CYMBAL SWEET SPOT

The ride cymbal can be played on the bell (the raised center of the cymbal) or on the bow. The sweet spot I'm referring to is on the bow about two-thirds in from the edge. This point gives you the best stick definition and overall tone of the cymbal.

TRACK 13

If you play too near the edge of the ride cymbal, the stick definition decreases and the overall "wash" of the cymbal takes over.

TRACK 14

67 VARYING DEGREES OF SHUFFLE

A shuffle is obtained by leaving out the middle note of each three-note triplet group, and looks like this:

When playing an eighth-note shuffle, the first note will fall on the beat. The other note of the shuffle can be manipulated to change the shuffle's feel:

TRACK 15

This first track I consider to be a "deep pocket" shuffle, where the shuffled note is held back, and played much closer to the beat that immediately follows it.

TRACK 16

The other extreme would be to only slightly shuffle these hi-hat notes. In this track, the hi-hat is not really straight or totally shuffled. This is a hard feel to play consistently. Many of the early rock 'n' roll records had this feel because most of these drummers came from a jazz background and were used to swinging.

Depending on the song I'm playing, the feel may fall somewhere in between these. Experiment with this. It really changes the overall feel of a song.

68 HI-HAT SPLASHES

Besides hitting the hi-hat cymbals with sticks, you can also step on the pedal to achieve some different sounds. For the normal closed hi-hat, you would step on the pedal so that the cymbals close and produce a "chick" sound.

You can also let the cymbals "splash" together and continue to sustain. To achieve this splash effect, I use the heel of my foot to step on the pedal and then quickly lift it off (so the cymbals sustain). Using the heel allows a more direct hit on the pedal—rather than flexing at the ankle. You may have to turn your foot a little to the side in order to get your heel up further on the pedal.

TRACK 17

You can use this technique in grooves and fills.

TRACK 18

69 DON'T REINVENT THE WHEEL

You know the old saying, "Don't reinvent the wheel"? What it means is this: Someone before you has probably done what you're doing right now.

For me, subscribing to monthly drumming and music magazines is essential to my growth as a musician. Following the tips offered by pros in columns, articles, and interviews has helped me learn and grow as a player over the years. It's always interesting to get other drummers' views on playing, as well as to keep in touch with the new products available.

70 PACKING A COOLER

No, I'm not going to give you tips on how to pack a lunch, but rather to remind you to do so. Over the years of playing clubs and doing recording sessions, I've learned that packing a cooler with water, energy drinks, fruit, and other light snacks can help me get through the job.

Staying hydrated is always important, but when you're on stage under the hot lights, your body is going to need more to keep up with what you're sweating out. I began taking my own water to gigs because it can be hard to make it to the bar in a crowded club, and the bar water can sometimes taste pretty bad.

Snacking on breaks will help refuel your body for the rest of the gig.

71 THE PRACTICE KIT

If you are gigging or doing recording sessions on a regular basis, setting up and tearing down to practice for these can be a drag. If you can afford it, I'd suggest getting a practice drumset that you can leave set up at home or the rehearsal studio. It doesn't have to be "top of the line" just to practice.

Keep your "good" drumset packed up and ready to go at a moment's notice for those last minute fill-in calls. I even have different set-ups that I use for recording and playing in different bands. The ultimate is to have complete set-ups for all of your different situations (including cases and hardware).

72 MORE HI-HAT SOUNDS

Hi-hat cymbals are able to produce a variety of sounds. You probably know the basic ones: closed, half-open, and open. There are so many degrees of the half-open sound; experiment to find what fits the song best.

With the cymbals closed, you also have the choice of playing with the tip of the stick on the flat surface of the top cymbal for a lighter more articulate sound, or with the shoulder of the stick on the edge of the cymbals for a bigger sound.

Also keep in mind the sounds you can make with just your foot on the pedal. These can vary from closed to open "splashes," too. Listen to all of these hi-hat sound variations on the following track.

TRACK 19

73 SYMPATHETIC SNARE BUZZ

The snare drum gets its name from the spiraled wires touching the bottom head. Because this bottom head is very thin, it tends to resonate easily, and nearby toms can set it into motion, causing the snares to buzz. This is quite typical and mostly unavoidable. Although a little snare buzz is tolerable, too much can be annoying.

You may find that one particular tom sets the snares off more than another. This is because both the tom heads and the snare-side head are resonating at a very similar frequency. One remedy is to either tune the snare-side head or the tom heads differently. Another is to detune the four tension rods closest to the snares on the snare drum's bottom head. This basically reduces the snare's sensitivity, but can alleviate the annoying buzzing problem.

74 CUSTOM DRUM MIC SNAKE

If you play with a regular group and handle the PA yourselves, it's a great idea to make your own drum snake. After setting up your drums and placing the mics where they need to be on your set, plug the cables into the mics and run all of the mic cables together as a group to one side of your kit (to either a snake box or a mixer on stage). Once you have everything where you need it, use zip ties to connect all of your mic cables together to their custom length. Be sure to label the mic cable ends (i.e. kick, snare, tom 1, etc.) and leave enough slack for minor adjustments. You should now have your own custom drum snake to reduce the clutter around your kit as well as your set-up time.

75 ONE HEAD AT A TIME

When tuning double-headed drums, always mute the head you are not working on by setting the drum on a carpeted floor or a towel, in order to get each head in tune with itself. Then, pick up the drum buy the rim, and hit it to hear both heads resonating together for the overall sound of the drum.

76 TUNING IN ISOLATION

Always tune the drum you are working on away from your other drums, in order to hear that drum alone and more clearly. The other drums (and cymbals), if left on the kit, will resonate when you hit the drum you are working on and cloud your pitch reference, making it more difficult to tune.

A drum's hoops will affect its tuning, sound, and feel. Triple-flanged hoops are standard on most drums. They are made of steel, formed (bent) into shape, and welded.

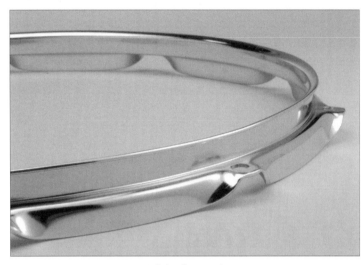

triple-flanged

Triple-flanged hoops can vary in thickness between manufacturers. They make hitting the drumhead more "giving" and "spongy-feeling," and can help disguise shell irregularities. When tuning, they are more forgiving, since they "give" slightly in relevance to the tension at each lug point. The thicker triple-flanged hoops can begin to take on die-cast hoop characteristics. Also, if your hoop is bent in any way, it will make tuning very difficult. You can either try bending it back to true, or replace it to get the most even tuning possible out of your drum.

Die-cast hoops are formed in a die and are very rigid. You will find these hoops on the more expensive snare drums and drum sets. Die-cast hoops have a feel that is quite the opposite of triple-flanged hoops. They make the drumhead feel much harder and more solid when hit in the center, and give a sharper attack to the sound. They also affect the overall tone of the drum. On toms, especially when tuned higher, they bring out a sort of "honk" quality; and in general, are less warm sounding.

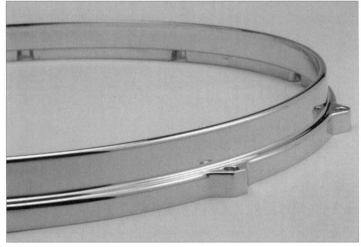

die-cast

 die-cast hoop (tom)

TRACK 20

On snare drums, die-cast hoops add more "crack" to rim shots, and make slamming backbeats feel much more solid.

 die-cast hoop (snare)

TRACK 21

The tuning of drums with die-cast hoops requires much more precision, since there is virtually no give to them. Since they are more rigid, turning one tension rod also will affect the adjacent lugs, and even the whole head in general. These hoops can make tuning trickier at first, but they definitely have an appealing quality to them.

Wood hoops have traditionally been used on bass drums, but, to keep costs down, many of the less expensive sets now use metal hoops. Some drum companies even offer wooden hoops on toms and snare drums. The wood hoops generally have a warmer sound, since they absorb some vibration when the drum is struck.

MAKING PLASTIC SNARE STRAPS

Most snares can be attached to the snare strainer and butt-side using plastic straps. Don't use shoestrings or leather straps, as they'll stretch and won't hold a constant tension. Nylon cord and steel cable are better for finely positioning the snares for lateral adjustment, but plastic straps are the easiest to install.

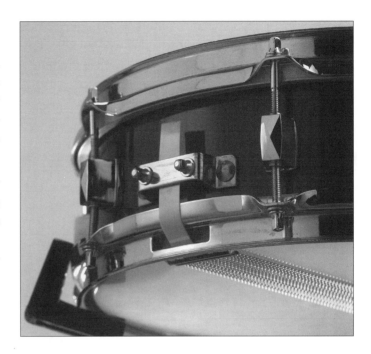

Here's a tip for reusing worn-out, single-ply drumheads: Cut your own plastic straps from them! They need to be about eight inches long and one-half inch wide. If nothing else, cut some for spares to throw in your gig toolbox just in case.

79
OWN GOOD GEAR

Buy the best gear you can afford, and keep it well maintained. With musical instruments, you do get what you pay for. Have what is appropriate for various playing situations. You wouldn't take a huge double bass kit to a jazz combo gig or a four-piece jazz kit to a heavy metal performance. Cymbal requirements can also change for different situations, so after buying the "standards" that work well in most cases, you may want some different specialty cymbals.

80 DRUMMER OR BUSINESSMAN?

The answer to the question is both! Being a freelance musician can have many rewards, but you'll still have to take care of the business side when you're not on stage. If you're in school, it would be advantageous to take some business courses to help prepare yourself.

Some areas you'll encounter: writing gig contracts, negotiating and getting paid for the gig, budgeting well for an inconsistent income, phone etiquette, promoting yourself with business cards and advertising, being your own accountant, figuring out your taxes, etc.

81 DRUM TUNING

When tuning any drum, the object is to first make sure each head is in tune with itself. To do this, tap the head with a stick about one inch from the hoop at each lug point. Pick the best-sounding pitch to you, and match the other lugs to it by tightening or loosening them. A simple way to help you hear the pitch at each lug is to touch the middle of the head with one finger.

Do not press hard, or it will raise the pitch of the head and defeat the purpose. This procedure controls overtones and clarifies the pitch, so you can better focus on each individual lug. Listen to the following demo to hear the tapping at the different lugs—first without touching the head, then the more focused sound when touching the center of the head with one finger.

TRACK 22

This is also a great way to tune the batter heads quickly when on a gig, without taking the drums off the mount or stand.

On toms, tune both heads the same, or the bottom head a little higher.

82 SHORTHAND CHARTS

If you need to learn songs quickly, write out your own shorthand charts. Listen to the song, count the number of measures of each section, and list them on a piece of paper, something like this:

Intro	8 measures (drums enter with a fill in meas. 4)
Verse 1	8 measures
Pre-Chorus	8 measures
Chorus	12 measures
Bridge	8 measures
Verse 2	8 measures
Pre-Chorus	8 measures
Chorus	12 measures
Bridge	4 measures
Gtr. Solo	16 measures
Verse 3	8 measures
Pre-Chorus	8 measures
Chorus	16 measures
Ending	Crash on beat 1 and let ring

You can also get more detailed and write out the basic beat for each section, or any specific fills.

83 GAINING EXPERIENCE

The best way to get better at anything is to do it a lot. Drumming is no different. Play with as many musicians as you can. Don't limit yourself. I once had a friend who played in six different bands at one time! Always try to play with musicians that are better than you to learn from them. Even if the pay isn't very good in some situations, you'll still gain valuable experience.

If you're learning a new style of music, ask someone that knows the style well to give you their Top 10 list of CDs in that style, then go out and buy a few.

To assist you in becoming a more well-rounded drummer, the following tips (#84–101) offer sample grooves in various popular styles. There are many variations to the grooves shown here, but they are a place to start to better understand these styles.

84 ROCK 'N' ROLL

Rock 'n' roll began in the '50s and drew from a variety of styles—mainly blues, R&B, and country, but also gospel, jazz, and folk.

A quarter-note pulse in the snare and bass drum creates a driving beat.

TRACK 23

This is as basic as rock 'n' roll gets, but you still need to play it with conviction.

TRACK 24

This is considered "four on the floor" because of the quarter-note bass drum pattern. The two consecutive snare hits on 2 and & are also a characteristic of early rock 'n' roll grooves.

TRACK 25

To change it up, early rock 'n' roll drummers would occasionally play the tom-tom as part of the groove, too.

TRACK 26

Because early rock 'n' roll was born out of the '50s, many of the drummers were accustomed to playing jazz prior to this new style—so many of their beats were triplet-based, or shuffled.

TRACK 27

TRACK 28

85 COUNTRY

The following classic country grooves may prove harder than they look. The object is to make them fall "in the pocket" with the bass player.

The first is the two-beat feel with the accented snare hitting on the upbeats.

TRACK 29

The next groove is known as the "train beat." Be sure to play the accents for authenticity. It can be played with sticks, brushes, or multi-rods.

TRACK 30

This one uses an alternating shuffle pattern on the snare.

TRACK 31

This Texas swing groove should be played with fairly heavy accents on 2 and 4.

TRACK 32

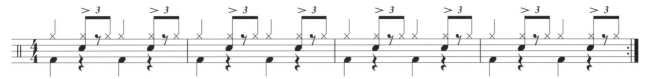

The last example is a straight-ahead country shuffle.

TRACK 33

86 GOSPEL

The upbeat tempo of these gospel grooves makes them fun to play. Just make sure that the offbeat kick pattern in the second measure falls into the pocket. Another challenge is to only accent beats 2 and 4 on the snare drum and not along with the bass drum pattern.

TRACK 34

TRACK 35

SOUL

Soul is a type of R&B—typically smoother, slicker, and a bit more commercial than pure rhythm 'n' blues.

The first example is a little more upbeat in tempo.

TRACK 36

This is a slower, more laid-back soul groove. Try to keep it smooth and flowing.

TRACK 37

The last example uses a little more syncopation between the kick and snare. Be sure to shuffle the sixteenth notes to add more "soul" to this groove.

TRACK 38

88 MOTOWN

The Motown sound was a bright, pop-oriented version of R&B. Although not every song used this, the signature Motown drum groove consisted of a quarter-note snare with the varying kick drum pattern. The quarter-note snare pattern really drove these beats.

TRACK 39

TRACK 40

SWING/JAZZ

These first two examples of swing are from the big band era and were typically played on the hi-hat. They seem deceivingly simple, but the trick lies in the feel of the swung triplet. The amount of "swing" will vary when playing this groove at different tempos.

TRACK 41

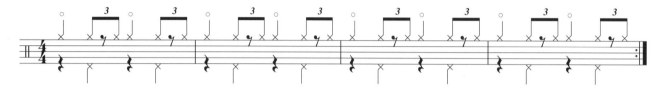

The quarter-note bass drum pattern on this example follows the walking bass lines of this style. The bass drum should be played much softer than the hi-hat.

TRACK 42

This is the most basic form of the jazz ride pattern. The hi-hat continues to keep time on 2 and 4 with the foot. When playing jazz, the ride cymbal and foot hi-hat are the most important parts. The snare and bass drum are used to accentuate and "kick" musical phrases, rather than being the foundation of the groove.

TRACK 43

The bass drum is sometimes used as part of the groove if played very softly.

TRACK 44

90 BLUES

The blues is played with a strong shuffle feel, with the snare accenting the backbeats on 2 and 4.

TRACK 45

Ghost notes have quite an effect on the blues shuffle sound. This next groove is called a "double shuffle" because both hands play the same thing.

TRACK 46

This one also uses ghost notes. Be sure to play them soft, and 2 and 4 accented.

TRACK 47

Another popular blues groove is the 12/8 feel. The shuffle is now shared between the kick and snare.

TRACK 48

91 HARD ROCK

Hard rock from the late '60s through the '80s could be described as loud, simple, and driving. The main elements of hard rock drumming are the kick and snare—these should be played the loudest (as opposed to in jazz, where the ride and hi-hat set the pulse).

TRACK 49

TRACK 50

TRACK 51

54

92 PUNK

Punk drum grooves can look simple when written out but are difficult to play fast. To consistently play at these fast tempos, without dragging—over the course of a song or set—can take a lot of stamina.

TRACK 52

TRACK 53

TRACK 54

MODERN METAL

Modern metal drumming is more complex and syncopated than hard rock. The grooves can be quite aggressive with busier kick drum patterns.

The first groove rides on the crash cymbal, which produces a "shhh" sound.

TRACK 55

This example shows the more syncopated kick drum typical to this style.

TRACK 56

94 FUNK

In the late '60s, soul, R&B, gospel, and rock mixed to form a new style called funk. What makes funk beats so "funky" are the offbeat snare hits, ghost notes, and open hi-hats. Funk beats are generally quite syncopated and use a lot of sixteenth-based rhythms.

TRACK 57

TRACK 58

TRACK 59

95 DISCO

Disco originated from the groove-oriented sound of the '70s and funk. Disco is all about keeping a simple beat to dance to. A frequent sound is the open and closed hi-hat. The four-on-the-floor bass drum pattern gives these grooves their driving pulse.

TRACK 60

TRACK 61

TRACK 62

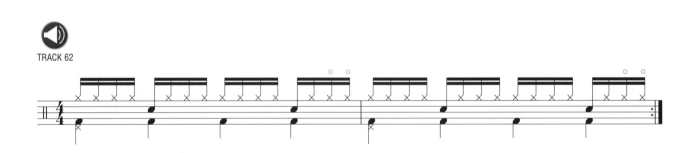

96 NEW ORLEANS

The second-line street beats were originally played by a snare drummer and a bass drummer (part of a nine-piece brass band) while marching in the street. "Second line" refers to the people who walked and danced behind the band following a funeral. These were upbeat songs that signified rejoice that the deceased was now in a better place. These beats were later adapted to the drumset. There are quite a few variations to these depending on tempo and the use of open (double-stroke) or closed (buzz) rolls. The following are a few basic grooves to get you started.

TRACK 63

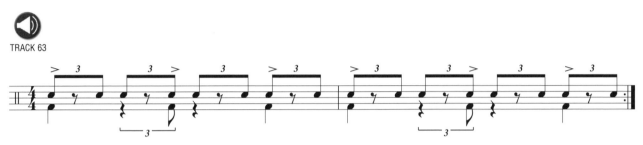

TRACK 64

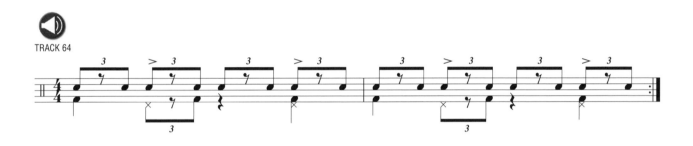

TRACK 65

97 HIP-HOP

Hip-hop is a type of funk that evolved from rap music. Many times, these beats are put together on a drum machine or constructed from drum loops. However, they can also be played on an acoustic drumset, too. You'll notice a close resemblance of these beats to some funk grooves. The differences between the two would lie in the lyrics, instrumentation, and drum sounds more than the actual beat.

TRACK 66

TRACK 67

98 SAMBA

The samba is Brazilian in origin. It uses a repeating pattern (called an ostinato) in the feet. The right hand can play on the flat surface or bell of the ride, or on a cowbell. There are many samba variations; try these for starters.

TRACK 68

TRACK 69

BOSSA NOVA

The bossa nova is a very common Latin groove. Its cross-stick pattern is based off the Latin clave rhythm ($| \quad |$ or $| \quad |$). Notice the same ostinato bass drum pattern as the samba.

TRACK 70

TRACK 71

MAMBO

The mambo is a Cuban dance that became popular in the '50s. The right hand should be played on a cowbell, but you could substitute the ride cymbal bell if you don't have one.

TRACK 72

TRACK 73

101 REGGAE

Reggae is a dance music that made its roots in Jamaica. When playing reggae, the strong beat is on beat 3. The grooves can be straight or shuffled. Try these grooves to start with.

TRACK 74

TRACK 75

TRACK 76

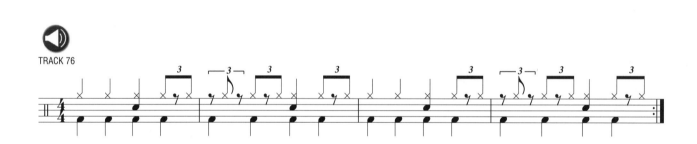